U.S. Regions

The People of the
Southeast

Blaine Wiseman

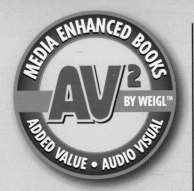

AV² provides enriched content that supplements and complements this book Weigl's AV² books strive to create inspired learning and engage young mind in a total learning experience.

Your AV² Media Enhanced books come alive with...

Audio
Listen to sections of the book read aloud.

Key Words
Study vocabulary, and complete a matching word activity.

Video
Watch informative video clips.

Quizzes
Test your knowledge.

Embedded Weblinks
Gain additional information for research.

Slide Show
View images and captions, and prepare a presentation.

Try This!
Complete activities and hands-on experiments.

... and much, much more!

Go to **www.av2books.com**, and enter this book's unique code.

BOOK CODE

K 7 8 1 7 2 7

AV² by Weigl brings you media enhanced books that support active learning.

Published by AV² by Weigl
350 5th Avenue, 59th Floor
New York, NY 10118

Websites: www.av2books.com   www.weigl.com

Library of Congress Control Number: 2014942102

ISBN 978-1-4896-2462-8 (hardcover)
ISBN 978-1-4896-2463-5 (softcover)
ISBN 978-1-4896-2464-2 (single-user eBook)
ISBN 978-1-4896-2465-9 (multi-user eBook)

Printed in the United States of America in North Mankato, Minnesota
1 2 3 4 5 6 7 8 9 18 17 16 15 14

062014
WEP060614

Project Coordinator: Aaron Carr
Design: Mandy Christiansen

Every reasonable effort has been made to trace ownership and to obtain permission to reprint copyright material. The publishers would be pleased to have any errors or omissions brought to their attention so that they may be corrected in subsequent printings.

Weigl acknowledges Getty Images as its primary image supplier for this title.

Contents

Introducing the Southeast

Today, the Southeast is one of the most populated regions in the United States. From the 1500s, adventurers and explorers began to arrive in the area. These Europeans came from South America, sailing north via the Gulf of Mexico. They also came from Europe, sailing across the Atlantic Ocean. Making contact with the American Indian groups already living there means the region has been an important crossroads for many different groups.

Washington

Oregon

Montana

Idaho

Wyoming

Nevada

Utah

California

Colorado

Arizona

New Mexico

Pacific Ocean

MEXICO

Legend

- West (11 states)
- Southwest (5 states)
- Northeast (11 states)
- Southeast (11 states)
- Midwest (12 states)

Alaska

0   500 Miles
0   500 Km

Hawai'i

0   100 Miles
0   100 Km

Where People Live in the Southeast

Compare the populations of the biggest city in each Southeastern state.

City	Population
Jacksonville, **Florida**	836,507
Charlotte, **North Carolina**	775,202
Memphis, **Tennessee**	655,155
Louisville, **Kentucky**	605,110

City	Population
Virginia Beach, **Virginia**	447,021
Atlanta, **Georgia**	443,775
New Orleans, **Louisiana**	369,250
Birmingham, **Alabama**	212,038

City	Population
Jackson, **Mississippi**	175,437
Columbia, **South Carolina**	131,686
Charleston, **West Virginia**	51,018

*2012 population figures

Settling the Southeast

The Southeast's location, climate, and abundance of natural resources make it an attractive place for people to live. Many American Indian groups originally lived in the area in settlements along the Mississippi River. These groups were named after the river and are known as the **Mississippian culture**. Later, explorers sailed to Southeastern shores from South America and Europe. They were soon followed by thousands more Europeans. African slaves were also brought to the region by European landowners.

In the 20th century, many more people arrived in the area. These people came to the Southeast from the Caribbean, as well as Central and South America. These migrants were looking for both freedom and work.

The Cherokee American Indians are believed to be descended from the Mississippian culture.

Southeastern Migrations

1565–1710

In 1565, the Spanish formed the colony of St. Augustine, Florida. Europeans began flooding into North America. More and more English colonies were formed from Florida up to North Carolina.

1619–1778

Many of the people living in English colonies were slaves. The practice of slavery grew, and by the time the United States became a nation, there were about 400,000 slaves in the Southeastern colonies.

1755

Louisiana is famous for its Cajun culture. Cajun comes from the word "Acadian," a French-speaking culture from Canada. In 1755, the English forced about 7,000 Acadians to leave Canada. Many made their way to Louisiana, where they received a warm welcome.

1960s–1970s

Florida is only 100 miles (160 km) from the island of Cuba. After the Cuban Revolution, many Cubans started migrating to the United States. Between 1965 and 1973, more than 200,000 Cuban **refugees** were brought to Miami. Today, 1.4 million people of Cuban descent live in Florida.

1970s–present

Southeastern states such as Florida, Georgia, and South Carolina are popular destinations for "Snowbirds." These are retired people who travel south from colder northern states and Canada. Most of these people only stay for the season. This migration brings about 800,000 people to Florida every winter.

Historic Events

Long before the United States became a country, many important historical events had taken place in the Southeast. This region has played an important role in American history. Through wars and revolutions, discoveries and disasters, people and events of the Southeast have helped shape the history of the United States.

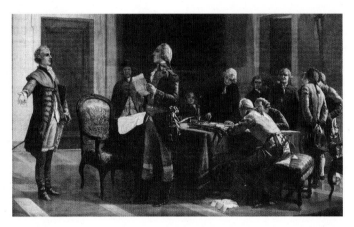

American Independence (1775–1783)

Throughout the 1700s, the British created colonies along the Atlantic coast. These included North Carolina, South Carolina, and Georgia. In 1775, thirteen of these colonies began fighting for their independence from Great Britain. As a result of the war, the United States of America was formed, and the Thirteen Colonies became the first states.

Oil Spill (2010)

When an oil rig in the Gulf of Mexico exploded, 11 people were killed, and oil began leaking into the water. For nearly 100 days, the oil kept flowing into the Gulf. The oil slick polluted more than 600 miles (965 kilometers) of coastline, and more than 52,500 square miles (135,974 square km) of water was closed to fishing.

The Confederacy (1861–1865)

In the 1860s, slave labor was an important part of the economy in the South. When the north wanted to **abolish** slavery, 11 states decided to leave the Union, leading to the Civil War. The Confederate States included the Southeastern states of Florida, Mississippi, Georgia, Alabama, Louisiana, South Carolina, North Carolina, and Tennessee.

Civil Rights Movement (1950s and 1960s)

Led by activists such as Dr. Martin Luther King, Jr. and Rosa Parks, millions of African Americans began to protest for their rights. In 1964, the Civil Rights Act ended **segregation**. In 1965, African Americans were given equal voting rights.

Hurricane Katrina (2005)

Hurricane Katrina was the worst natural disaster in U.S. history. While the storm was powerful, the biggest danger came from water rushing in from the Gulf of Mexico. A series of **levees** around New Orleans failed, and 80 percent of the city was flooded. The storm and flood caused $108 billion in damage and killed almost 2,000 people.

620,000 people were killed fighting in the Civil War.

The 2010 oil spill leaked 206 million gallons (779 million liters) of oil into the Gulf of Mexico. That is enough oil to fill more than 300 Olympic swimming pools.

Historic Southeasterners

Many explorers, activists, athletes, and entertainers are from the Southeast. These well-known Southeasterners have made a huge impact on the history and culture of their region and all over the world.

Helen Keller (1880-1968)

Helen Keller was born in Tuscumbia, Alabama. When she was just 18 months old, she lost her sight and hearing. With the help of a special teacher, Anne Sullivan, Keller learned to read, write, and speak. She then worked to help people with disabilities. Keller was awarded the Presidential Medal of Freedom in 1964. This medal is awarded each year by the president to people who make an outstanding contribution to society.

Jesse Owens (1913–1980) Jesse Owens was born in Oakville, Alabama, where he worked in his father's cotton fields. He was a high school and college track and field star. He went on to compete in the 1936 Olympics in Berlin, Germany. There, he won four gold medals for three sprinting events and the long jump. Owens fast became a hero all around the world.

Owens' real name was **James Cleveland Owens,** and his family called him **"J.C."** When he went to a new school, a teacher did not understand his southern accent. She thought he introduced himself as **"Jesse,"** and the name stuck.

Jackie Robinson (1919–1972)

Jackie Robinson was born in Cairo, Georgia. He served in the United States Army during World War II. After the war, he began playing baseball in a professional league for African Americans. His speed and skill soon caught the eye of the Brooklyn Dodgers. In 1947, Robinson became the first African American to play in the major leagues. He was named National League Most Valuable Player in 1949, and a World Series champion in 1955. Throughout his life, he fought for civil rights.

Jackie Robinson's older brother, Matthew Robinson, won a silver medal at the 1936 Olympics, finishing second to Jesse Owens.

Martin Luther King, Jr. (1929–1968)

Dr. Martin Luther King, Jr. was born in Atlanta, Georgia. Dr. King was a powerful speaker who became the leader of the Civil Rights movement in the United States. His protests and speeches, including the famous "I Have a Dream" speech, helped African Americans gain **equality**. King was **assassinated** in Memphis, Tennessee, in 1968.

Elvis Presley (1935–1977)

Elvis Presley was born in Tupelo, Mississippi. He got his first guitar at the age of 10. In 1955, he released his first hit, *Heartbreak Hotel*, and became a star. With his good looks and popularity, he was soon starring in movies such as *Love Me Tender* and *Blue Hawaii*. Almost 40 years after his death, "The King of Rock 'n' Roll" is still one of the most popular musicians in the world.

Jim Henson (1936-1990)

Growing up in Greenville, Mississippi, Jim Henson had a passion for puppets. Henson got a job on a new show called *Sesame Street*. In 1976, he created another hit, *The Muppet Show*. Henson's characters, such as Kermit the Frog, Miss Piggy, Big Bird, and Cookie Monster are still popular with children and adults all over the world.

Cultural Groups

The Southeast is often considered the most cultural region in the United States. Many different cultures have blended together to create unique Southeastern traditions. The region's history of Spanish, French, and English rule have had a major impact. Some of the traditions and practices of these cultures are still visible today. A long history of slavery and segregation in this region has helped build a strong African American culture. Southeastern cultures have had an impact on the entire United States and in other countries all over the world.

Mardi Gras is a popular French festival with floats, parades, dance, and music in the streets. The French Quarter of New Orleans is famous for its Mardi Gras celebrations.

Cultural Communities

Segregation created many African American neighborhoods across the region, but the Southeast is home to many other cultures as well.

Little Havana, Miami, Florida

By 1980, more than 95,000 Cubans were living in an area of Miami that became known as Little Havana. These migrants set up a colorful community as more and more people moved from Cuba during the 1960s and 1970s.

Sweet Auburn, Atlanta, Georgia

Sweet Auburn is a historic African American community in Atlanta. It became a center of African American culture where former slaves and their families built homes and businesses. This district is the birthplace of Dr. Martin Luther King, Jr.

Melrose Park, Florida

For decades, millions of Jamaicans have left their island country to live in the United States. Most of these migrants have settled in Florida. The neighborhood of Melrose Park in Fort Lauderdale is the biggest Jamaican community in the United States. More than 80 percent of the neighborhood's residents are African American.

French Quarter, New Orleans, Louisiana

New Orleans' famous French Quarter was founded in 1718. Despite its name, French is only one of many cultures to influence the area. Spanish rule brought Spanish culture and architecture. At the beginning of the 20th century, the area became well-known for its jazz musicians and other African American influences.

Major Cities of the Southeast

While much of the Southeast is made up of rural communities, it is also home to many big cities. These major cities are centers of history and culture. They also play a major role in the economy of the United States.

Miami is not Florida's biggest city, or the capital, but it is the major economic and cultural center of the state. Before the 20th century, it was only a small village. Even through most of the 1900s, Miami was more of a tourist destination than a major city. Today, it is home to many large finance companies. It is also a travel **hub** for flights and cruises to the Caribbean and Latin America.

Louisville is best known for its famous horse race, the Kentucky Derby. It is more than a one-horse town, however. The biggest city in Kentucky is a mix of tradition and progress, with a growing economy and a strong tourism industry. Its low cost of living, along with a strong business community, makes Louisville a fast-growing city.

New Orleans is located at the southern edge of the continent, but it is central to business in the United States. Louisiana's biggest city is located at the mouth of the Mississippi River. This gives ships easy access from the Gulf of Mexico to more than half of the United States. Along with its business strength, "The Big Easy" is one of the most popular tourist destinations in the United States.

Charlotte, North Carolina, is located where an inland sea port meets busy highways and railroads. This location has made it one of the strongest cities in the U.S. for business. Despite this, "The Queen City" has kept its historical and cultural identity.

Georgia's capital city Atlanta is also its biggest. Many large companies, such as Coca-Cola, UPS, Delta Airlines, and Home Depot call Atlanta home. This diverse business community has helped the city grow into one of America's most popular cities for job seekers.

State Capitals

The state capital is where the state government is situated. Political leaders make important decisions in these cities. These decisions affect their states, their region, and the entire United States.

State Capitals	Population
Nashville, **Tennessee**	624,496
Atlanta, **Georgia**	443,775
Raleigh, **North Carolina**	423,179
Baton Rouge, **Louisiana**	230,058
Richmond, **Virginia**	210,309
Montgomery, **Alabama**	205,293
Tallahassee, **Florida**	186,971
Jackson, **Mississipi**	175,437
Columbia, **South Carolina**	131,686
Charleston, **West Virginia**	51,018
Frankfort, **Kentucky**	27,590

*2012 population figures

Industries of the Southeast

Throughout its history, the economy of the Southeast has relied on natural resources and agriculture. Large deposits of resources such as coal, vast forests, and plenty of farmland drove the economy. Today, many of these industries are still important to the region, while new ones have also moved in. Manufacturing has become a major industry across the Southeast.

Alabama

Alabama is the country's third largest supplier of broilers. These young chickens are sold as food, and make up 60 percent of the state's agriculture industry.

- **40,000 jobs** in the state's poultry industry.
- **Generates $2.9 billion** per year for the state.

Louisiana

Louisiana is the third largest producer of oil and gas in the United States.

- About **$86,000 per year**—the average earnings for a Louisiana oil and gas worker.

Florida

Florida is the most popular tourist destination in the entire world. In 2013, 94.7 million people visited "The Sunshine State."

- **1 million** people work in Florida's tourism industry
- **$67 billion**—industry earnings in 2011

Virginia

Virginia has a diverse agriculture industry. Livestock such as broilers, beef, and turkey, along with crops such as soybeans are major parts of the state's agriculture.

- **311,000 jobs**
- **$52 billion per year**

Georgia

Georgia is known as "The Peach State," but it also produces many other crops. Transport of products such as broilers, eggs, and peanuts to other states is one of the Georgia's biggest industries.

- **352,000 Georgians** work in agricultural transportation.
- Generates **$66.9 billion** every year.

South Carolina

Forestry is one of South Carolina's biggest industries. About 68 percent of South Carolina's land is covered by forests.

- **90,624 forestry** jobs in the state.
- Brings more than **$17.4 billion** into the state per year.

Tennessee

Manufacturing is one of Tennessee's leading industries, creating more than 11 percent of the jobs in the state. There are more than 6,000 manufacturing plants in the state.

- **297,700 jobs** in Tennessee's manufacturing industry.
- **Contributes about $40 billion** to the state economy annually.

Mississippi

Mississippi is a major agricultural state, with more than 42,000 farms. Poultry and egg farming are the biggest parts of the industry.

- **29 percent** of Mississippi's workforce are employed by the agriculture industry.
- **Earnings of $7.4 billion in 2013**

West Virginia

Mining, especially coal, is a major part of West Virginia's economy. Coal mining makes up 75 percent of the state's mining revenue.

- **30,000 jobs**
- **$3.5 billion per year**

North Carolina

North Carolina's textile manufacturing industry turns cotton into fabric for clothing. It is one of the major industries, with 325 textile manufacturing companies in the state.

- **30,791 jobs in state's textile manufacturing** industry in 2012
- **$45,340**—the salary of an average worker in North Carolina's textile manufacturing industry.

Kentucky

Kentucky is a major U.S. manufacturer of cars. It is home to more than 400 facilities related to automotive manufacturing for some of the biggest car companies in the United States.

- **More than 82,000 jobs**
- **Exports totaled $4.4 billion in 2012**

Southeastern Tourism

The Southeast is a very popular region for tourism. Some of the country's most beautiful natural areas are found in the Southeast, including beaches and national parks. Historical treasures and cultural activities also attract many visitors to the region.

Georgia, Just 10 miles (16 km) from downtown Atlanta, Stone Mountain features a carving of Confederate leaders. It is a huge rock more than 5 miles (8 km) around. Visitors can walk to the top or take a cable car. About 4 million people enjoy the wide and exciting views of Stone Mountain Park every year.

Alabama, In 1970, Huntsville, Alabama, became the rocket base for the U.S. space program. At the United States Space & Rocket Center, tourists can see rockets, moon rocks, and many other space-related **artifacts**. More than half a million people visit the museum every year.

South Carolina, Myrtle Beach is a town on the Grand Strand, a string of communities on South Carolina's coast. Every summer, the population grows from 30,000 people to more than 350,000. More than 13 million people visit Myrtle Beach every year.

Kentucky, Mammoth Cave National Park is a 52,830 acre (21,380 hectare) area of forest, but its main attraction is what lies underneath. The park is home to the longest cave system in the world. Almost 400 miles (643 km) of the caves have been explored, and more caves are found every year. The park hosts 650,000 visitors each year, and 400,000 of them visit the caves.

Tennessee, Nashville is known as "Music City," but Tennessee's most famous piece of music history is in Memphis. Graceland was the home of Elvis Presley from 1957 until his death in 1977. Today, it is a museum dedicated to the life of "The King." Every year, Graceland hosts more than 600,000 Elvis fans.

Mississippi, In 1863, 77,000 Union soldiers attacked 33,000 Confederate soldiers in Vicksburg, Mississippi. Today, the area is a national military park. It covers more than 1,800 acres (728 hectares), surrounding the original battlefield. Each year, between 500,000 and 1 million people visit the park's walking trails, museum and monuments.

North Carolina, Great Smoky Mountains National Park covers 800 square miles (2,072 square km) in the Appalachian Mountains. Just over half of the park is in North Carolina, while the other part is in Tennessee. It is the most visited national park in the United States, with more than 9 million visitors bringing $718 million to the area every year.

Famous Southeasterners

The Southeast is a region of action, activism, culture, and competition. Its most famous people have been influenced by the legacies of the entertainers, leaders, and champions who have come before them.

Jasper Johns was born in 1930 in Augusta, Georgia, and raised in South Carolina. He always knew he wanted to be an artist. In the 1950s, Johns created a new style that would influence many artists after him. He uses regular, everyday items in his art, such as maps, cans, and the U.S. flag. Johns has become one of the best-known artists in the United States.

Morgan Freeman was born in Memphis in 1937. He spent most of his childhood in Mississippi, where he acted in many school plays. Freeman has become one of the most respected actors in the world. He won an Academy Award for his role in the movie *Million Dollar Baby*. His other roles include playing Nelson Mandela in the movie *Invictus* and being the voice for the documentary *March of the Penguins*.

Clarence Thomas was born in Pin Point, Georgia, in 1948. After Dr. Martin Luther King's assassination in 1968, Thomas was inspired to become a civil rights activist and lawyer. In 1991, he was appointed to the Supreme Court. Thomas became the second African American Supreme Court Justice.

Cassius Clay was born in 1942, in Louisville, Kentucky. In 1964, he changed his name to Muhammad Ali. He had already won an Olympic gold medal and the World Heavyweight title. Not only a fighter in the ring, Ali also fought for civil rights. He is known as one of the most charming, outspoken, and popular athletes in history. "The Greatest of All Time" is a hero to people all over the world.

Dolly Parton was born in Locust Ridge, Tennessee, in 1946. She sang in church and started performing at the age of 10. When she was only 13, Parton performed at the Grand Ole Opry. She has also acted in several movies. "The Queen of Country Music" has won seven Grammy Awards and has been nominated for two Academy Awards.

Michael Jordan was born in 1963 and grew up in Wilmington, North Carolina. Jordan led the University of North Carolina to the National Championship before joining the NBA, where he kept on winning. He won six NBA Championships and five Most Valuable Player (MVP) awards. Michael Jordan is often considered the greatest basketball player of all time.

Stephen Colbert is a comedian who grew up in Charleston, South Carolina. After working on *The Daily Show*, his political humor led to his own show, *The Colbert Report*. In 2014, Colbert was chosen to replace David Letterman as the new host of *The Late Show*. He has won six Emmy Awards and two Grammy Awards.

In 1986, **Dolly Parton** opened her own theme park, called **Dollywood**, in Pigeon Ford, Tennessee. Dollywood attracts **2.5 million visitors** every year.

Dale Earnhardt, Jr. was born in Kannapolis, North Carolina, in 1974. His grandfather and father were both successful NASCAR drivers, and Dale followed in their footsteps. At 17, he began racing cars, and five years later, became a NASCAR driver. While his dad is considered one of the greatest drivers of all time, Dale Jr. is NASCAR's most popular.

In 2001, *Dale Earnhardt Sr. was killed in a crash on the last turn of the last lap at the Daytona 500. Three years later,* **Dale Jr.** *raced at Daytona in his dad's honor.* **He won the race!**

Southeastern Politics

Politics have been a major part of life in the Southeast throughout U.S. history. The people of the region have always played a major role, and shown great interest, in national politics. Some of the greatest politicians in the United States have come from the Southeast.

George Washington was born in 1732 in Westmoreland County, Virginia, and lived much of his life at Mount Vernon. When the American Revolution began, Washington became the commander of the Continental Army, leading the Thirteen Colonies to independence. He became the first president of the United States of America in 1789.

Thomas Jefferson was born in 1743 in Shadwell, Virginia, and lived at the famous Monticello estate. Jefferson helped write the Declaration of Independence, was the first secretary of state, second vice president, and third president of the United States. As president, he doubled the size of the country with the Louisiana Purchase.

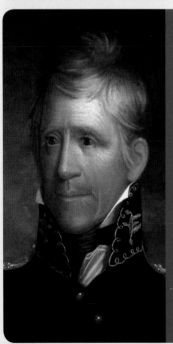

Andrew Jackson was born in an area between North and South Carolina in 1767. Fighting in the War of 1812, Jackson became a hero of the United States. After the war, he got involved in politics, founding the Democratic Party. "Old Hickory" served as president from 1829 until 1837.

Born in a Kentucky log cabin in 1809, Abraham Lincoln led the country through its most difficult time. The Civil War split the nation and killed more Americans than any other conflict. While he was assassinated before the war ended, Lincoln helped end slavery and reunite the United States.

State Politics

The Republican Party won nine of the eleven Southeastern states in the 2012 election. The closest result was in Florida, where President Obama won by 73,189 votes.

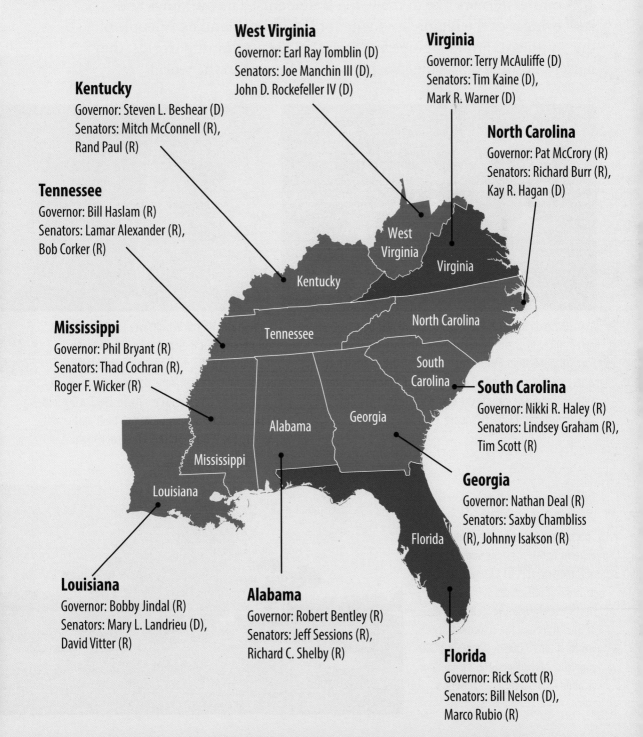

West Virginia
Governor: Earl Ray Tomblin (D)
Senators: Joe Manchin III (D),
John D. Rockefeller IV (D)

Virginia
Governor: Terry McAuliffe (D)
Senators: Tim Kaine (D),
Mark R. Warner (D)

Kentucky
Governor: Steven L. Beshear (D)
Senators: Mitch McConnell (R),
Rand Paul (R)

North Carolina
Governor: Pat McCrory (R)
Senators: Richard Burr (R),
Kay R. Hagan (D)

Tennessee
Governor: Bill Haslam (R)
Senators: Lamar Alexander (R),
Bob Corker (R)

Mississippi
Governor: Phil Bryant (R)
Senators: Thad Cochran (R),
Roger F. Wicker (R)

South Carolina
Governor: Nikki R. Haley (R)
Senators: Lindsey Graham (R),
Tim Scott (R)

Georgia
Governor: Nathan Deal (R)
Senators: Saxby Chambliss (R), Johnny Isakson (R)

Louisiana
Governor: Bobby Jindal (R)
Senators: Mary L. Landrieu (D),
David Vitter (R)

Alabama
Governor: Robert Bentley (R)
Senators: Jeff Sessions (R),
Richard C. Shelby (R)

Florida
Governor: Rick Scott (R)
Senators: Bill Nelson (D),
Marco Rubio (R)

Monuments and Buildings

Southeasterners like to make big statements. The buildings and bridges of the region are made for the unique land and people of the Southeast. From engineering wonders to entertaining worlds, they have built some of the biggest, tallest, and longest in the world.

At 4:30 am on April 12, 1861, the U.S. Civil War began at Fort Sumter, in Charleston Harbor, North Carolina. Today, Fort Sumter National Monument features the original fort, where visitors can learn all about the Civil War. Other sites at the monument include the Confederate Fort Moultrie and a museum at Liberty Square.

Orville and Wilbur Wright were not from the Southeast, but they made history in North Carolina in 1903. For four years, the brothers built and tested airplane designs at Kitty Hawk, where they had strong winds. In 1932, a 60-foot (18.3-meter) tall memorial was built at the spot where the Wright Brothers first took flight.

Towering over Walt Disney World is an 18-story sphere. Spaceship Earth is part of Disney's Experimental Prototype Community of Tomorrow (EPCOT). Completed in 1982, EPCOT covers 300 acres (121 hectares), showcasing technologies of the future and the cultures of the world. It took 3,000 designers, 10,000 construction workers, and $1.4 billion to build it over a three-year period.

The tallest building in the Southeast, Bank of America Plaza stands 1,023 feet (312 m) above Atlanta. It cost $150 million and only took 14 months to build the 55-story tower. While it is only the 10th tallest building in the United States, Bank of America Plaza is the tallest outside of New York or Chicago.

On the northern edge of New Orleans, the world's longest bridge over water stretches across Louisiana's biggest lake. The Lake Pontchartrain Causeway crosses almost 24 miles (38 km) of water. More than 40,000 cars cross the causeway every weekday.

Flags and Seals

Flags and seals display the symbols and values of the place they represent. Flags are planted in newly discovered lands, carried into battle, and flown at important sites. Seals are used for more official purposes, such as government buildings and legal documents.

Georgia

Flag Georgia's flag is based on the Confederate national flag. It has two vertical red bars on the top and bottom, surrounding a white middle bar. A blue square in the upper left features the state's **coat-of-arms**.

Seal The front of the seal features the state's coat-of-arms. The back has the words "Agriculture and Commerce", which is the state's **motto**.

North Carolina

Flag The North Carolina flag is red, white, and blue. These colors are based on the Confederate "Stars and Bars" flag.

Seal The seal has Lady Liberty and Plenty, representing freedom and agriculture.

South Carolina

Flag The crescent moon on the flag of South Carolina stands for glory. There is a palmetto tree as South Carolina is known as "The Palmetto State."

Seal The seal shows a palmetto tree over a broken oak tree. This represents a battle in the Revolutionary War, where British cannon balls bounced off Fort Sullivan's Palmetto log walls.

Mississippi

Flag Mississippi's flag takes its design from both the Union and Confederate flags. The red, white, and blue stripes are the same colors as the U.S. flag; St. Andrew's Cross and 13 stars represent the original 13 colonies of the United States.

Seal The seal shows an American eagle. An olive branch stands for peace and the arrows stand for power. There are 11 stars representing the 11 Confederate states.

Alabama

Flag Alabama's flag shows the St. Andrew's cross on a white background. St. Andrew's Cross was featured on the Confederate flag, and is also on the flags of Florida, Scotland, and Jamaica.

Seal The state seal shows a map of Alabama's nine major rivers and the surrounding states.

Tennessee

Flag The flag features three stars bound together by a circle showing the three Grand Divisions of Tennessee—East, Middle, and West.

Seal The state motto "Agriculture and Commerce" is shown on the seal. The Roman numerals "XVI" show that Tennessee was the 16th state in the Union.

Louisiana

Flag Louisiana's flag shows the state seal on a blue background.

Seal The seal shows a white pelican feeding its young pieces of its own flesh. The state bird is known for feeding its young this way when food is scarce.

Kentucky

Flag The state seal is featured in the middle of a blue background.

Seal The seal has the words "Commonwealth of Kentucky" on its outer rim. These words stand for Kentucky's **representative** government. The inner circle features the state motto, "United we stand, divided we fall."

Virginia

Flag The state seal is featured on a blue background.

Seal The front of the seal shows Virtus, the Roman goddess of bravery. The fallen man and crown stand for victory over the tyranny of Britain. The back shows the Roman goddesses of Liberty, Eternity, and Plenty.

West Virginia

Flag The flag shows the state seal surrounded by the state flower, rhododendron, on a white background with a blue border.

Seal The front of the seal shows a farmer, representing the agriculture industry. The miner represents the mining industry. The boulder with "June 20, 1863" shows the date West Virginia joined the Union.

Florida

Flag Florida's flag features the state seal over a red St. Andrew's Cross.

Seal The Florida seal shows the Sun's rays over the state tree, the Sabal palm, as well as a steamboat and a Seminole American Indian woman scattering flowers.

Challenges Facing the Southeast

Sinking Down

Coastal communities all over the world are threatened by rising sea levels. This rising water is caused by global warming. Glaciers and ice sheets in the Arctic and the Antarctic are melting, adding more water to the world's oceans. In the 20th century, the world's oceans rose by 8 inches (20 centimeters). They could rise as much as 6 feet (1.8 meters) in the 21st century.

The issue is even more serious in Louisiana. The Mississippi River Delta is a huge coastal wetland created by **sediment** dropped by the biggest river in the United States. Over time, this sediment settles and the land sinks. When people take groundwater and other resources from these areas, the land sinks even faster. Louisiana's coastal areas are sinking faster than sea levels are rising. The Coastal Master Plan is investing $25 billion to restore and build new land along the Louisiana coast. This will reduce flooding, and protect millions of people.

Blocking Off

One major factor causing the Mississippi River Delta to sink is happening hundreds or even thousands of miles (km) away. The Mississippi River flows 2,340 miles (3,765 km) from Minnesota to the Gulf of Mexico. Along the way, it carries million of tons (tonnes) of sediment to the Gulf every year. This sediment builds up, creating delta lands. The problem is that much more sediment never makes it to the end of the river.

★ Dams and levees help stop communities from flooding. They also give people water to drink and use for growing crops.

People have built more than 40,000 dams and levees along the Mississippi. Systems are also being built to carry sediment to the delta. In Louisiana, a new kind of diversion has been built to distribute sediment when it is needed most. This new technology releases sediment in different amounts at different times, allowing scientists to copy the natural flow. This way, delta lands can be rebuilt.

Since the 1850s, sediment in the Lower Mississippi River has decreased by **70 percent**.

Most sea levels in the U.S. rose by **1 foot** (30 cm) or less over the last century. Louisiana's sea levels rose by **3 to 4 feet** (90 to 120 cm).

Quiz

1 What two bodies of water border the Southeast?

2 Which country was responsible for building St. Augustine, Florida?

3 What was the worst natural disaster in the United States?

4 Who was the first African American to play in Major League Baseball?

5 Where is the biggest Jamaican-American community in the United States?

6 Which city is home to Coca-Cola?

8 In which state is "Graceland"?

9 What did Cassius Clay change his name to?

7 What state is home to more than 400 auto-related manufacturers?

10 Which president was born in a Kentucky log cabin?

ANSWERS: 1. The Atlantic Ocean and the Gulf of Mexico 2. Spain 3. Hurricane Katrina 4. Jackie Robinson 5. Melrose Park, Florida 6. Atlanta, Georgia 7. Kentucky 8. Tennessee 9. Muhammad Ali 10. Abraham Lincoln

Key Words

abolish: get rid of or make illegal

artifacts: items with historical or cultural meaning

assassinated: murdered for political reasons

coat-of-arms: a shield showing the symbols of a people or place

equality: being equal

hub: center

levees: walls that keep water out

Mississippian culture: mound-building American Indian cultures that lived in the 700–1800s in parts of what is now the Midwestern, Eastern, and Southeastern United States. These cultures grew crops such as corn, beans, and squash.

motto: a slogan or catch phrase

refugees: people who have been forced to leave their home by war or other disaster

representative: a government that works for the people

sediment: soil, dirt, rocks, and sand carried by water

segregation: the separation of black and white people in public areas

Index

Log on to www.av2books.com

AV[2] by Weigl brings you media enhanced books that support active learning. Go to www.av2books.com, and enter the special code found on page 2 of this book. You will gain access to enriched and enhanced content that supplements and complements this book. Content includes video, audio, weblinks, quizzes, a slide show, and activities.

AV[2] Online Navigation

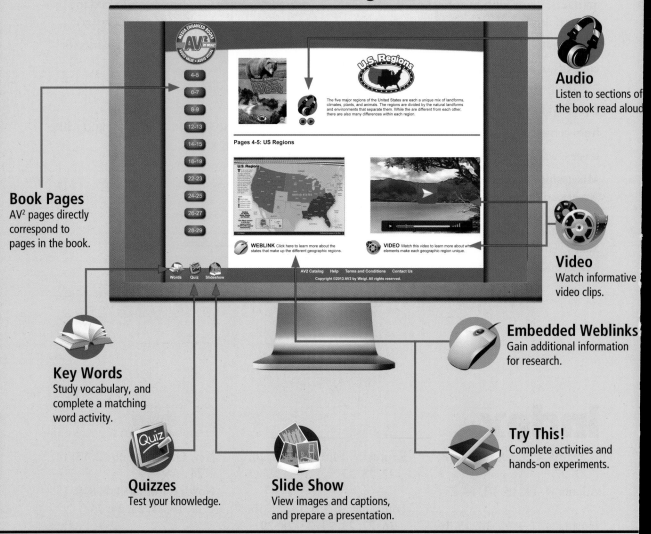

Book Pages
AV[2] pages directly correspond to pages in the book.

Audio
Listen to sections of the book read aloud

Video
Watch informative video clips.

Key Words
Study vocabulary, and complete a matching word activity.

Embedded Weblinks
Gain additional information for research.

Quizzes
Test your knowledge.

Slide Show
View images and captions, and prepare a presentation.

Try This!
Complete activities and hands-on experiments.

AV[2] was built to bridge the gap between print and digital. We encourage you to tell us what you like and what you want to see in the future.

Sign up to be an AV[2] Ambassador at www.av2books.com/ambassador.